Number Activities

Written by **Hanna Otero**

Illustrations by **Heidi Chang**

FlashKids

An imprint of Sterling Children's Books

This book belongs to

_____

FLASH KIDS, STERLING, and the distinctive Sterling logo are registered trademarks of
Sterling Publishing Co., Inc.

Published by Sterling Publishing Co., Inc.
387 Park Avenue South, New York, NY 10016
Text and illustrations © 2006 by Flash Kids
Distributed in Canada by Sterling Publishing
c/o Canadian Manda Group, 165 Dufferin Street
Toronto, Ontario, Canada M6K 3H6
Distributed in the United Kingdom by GMC Distribution Services
Castle Place, 166 High Street, Lewes, East Sussex, England BN7 1XU
Distributed in Australia by Capricorn Link (Australia) Pty. Ltd.
P.O. Box 704, Windsor, NSW 2756, Australia

Sterling ISBN 978-1-4114-3468-4

Manufactured in China

Lot #:
2 4 6 8 10 9 7 5 3 1
06/10

For information about custom editions, special sales, premium and
corporate purchases, please contact Sterling Special Sales
Department at 800-805-5489 or specialsales@sterlingpublishing.com.

Cover design and production by Mada Design, Inc.

Dear Parent,

Learning to count from one to ten is an important step for every child. *Number Activities* will help your child identify numbers and count to ten. The book includes counting activities, hidden pictures, number lines, and lots of practice with tracing and writing numbers. To get the most from *Number Activities*, follow these simple steps:

- Find a comfortable place where you and your child can work quietly.
- Help your child read the simple directions at the top of each activity.
- Encourage your child to go at his or her own pace. Offer lots of praise and support.
- Let your child reward his or her work with the included stickers.
- Most of all, remember that learning should be fun! Take time to color the pictures, talk about the activities, and enjoy this special time spent together.

1 One

1 big whale

Practice writing the number I.

I - - - - - - - - - - - - - - - -

- - - - - - - - - - - - - - - -

Practice writing the word **one**.

one - - - - - - - - - - - - -

- - - - - - - - - - - - - - - -

Circle the group of **I**.

Circle the group of **I**.

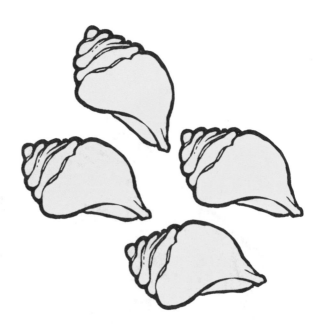

Find the hidden picture.

Color the spaces that show **I** dot.

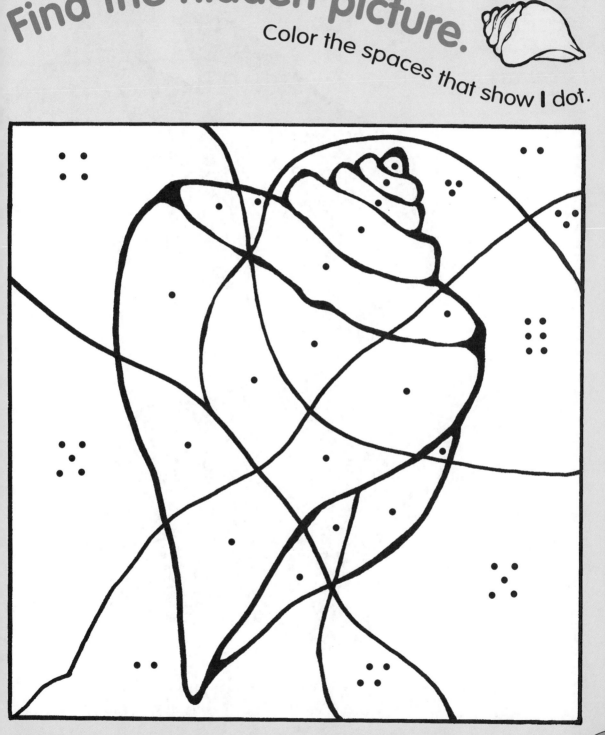

2 Two

2 sneaky sharks

Practice writing the number **2**.

2 — — — — — — — — — —

— — — — — — — — — — —

Practice writing the word **two**.

two — — — — — — — —

— — — — — — — — — — —

Circle the group of **2**.

Circle the group of **2**.

Find the hidden picture.

Color the spaces that show **2** dots.

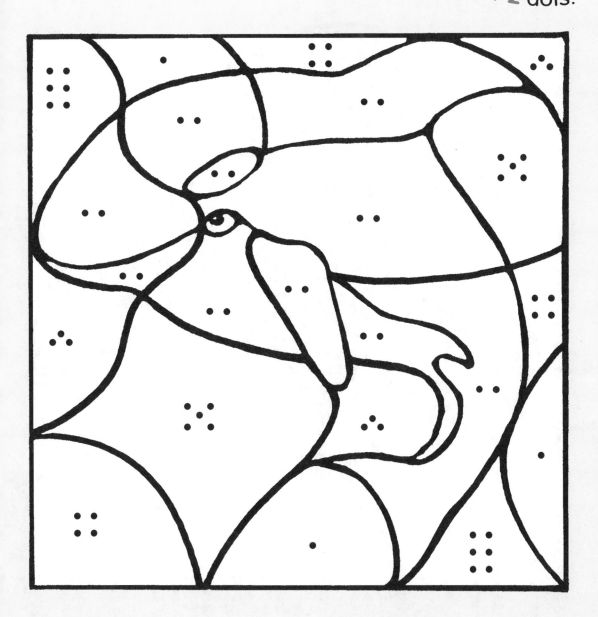

3 Three

3 diving dolphins

Practice writing the number **3**.

3 – – – – – – – – – – – – – – –

– – – – – – – – – – – – – – – – –

Practice writing the word **three**.

three – – – – – – – – – –

– – – – – – – – – – – – – – – – –

Circle the group of **3**.

Circle the group of **3**.

Find the hidden picture.

Color the spaces that show **3** dots.

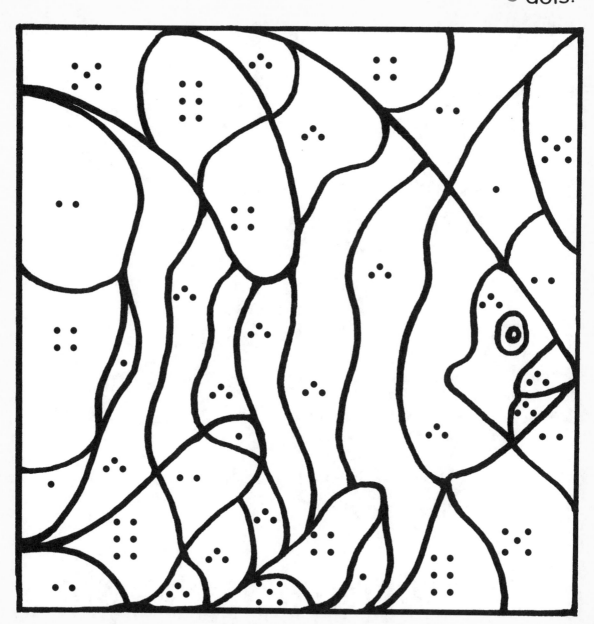

4 Four

4 swimming seals

Practice writing the number **4**.

4

Practice writing the word **four**.

four

Circle the group of **4**.

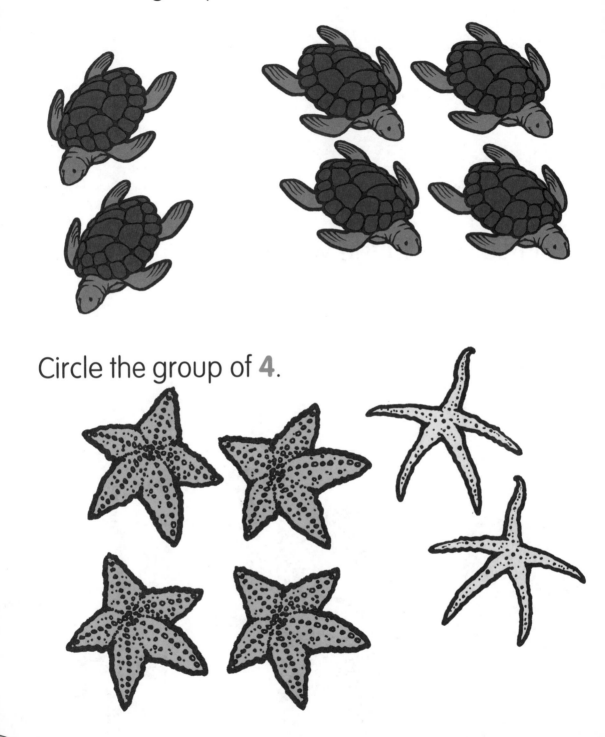

Circle the group of **4**.

Find the hidden picture.

Color the spaces that show **4** dots.

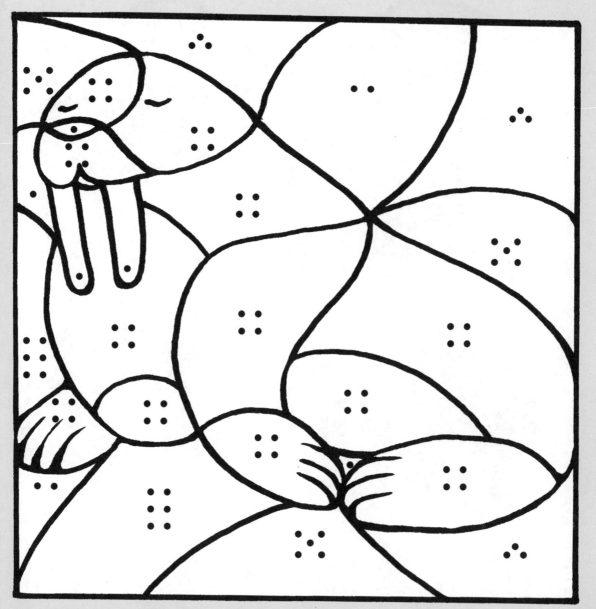

5 Five

5 fat fish

Practice writing the number 5.

5 – – – – – – – – – – – – – – –

– – – – – – – – – – – – – – – – –

Practice writing the word five.

five – – – – – – – – – – – – –

– – – – – – – – – – – – – – – – –

Circle the group of **5**.

Circle the group of **5**.

Find the hidden picture.

Color the spaces that show **5** dots.

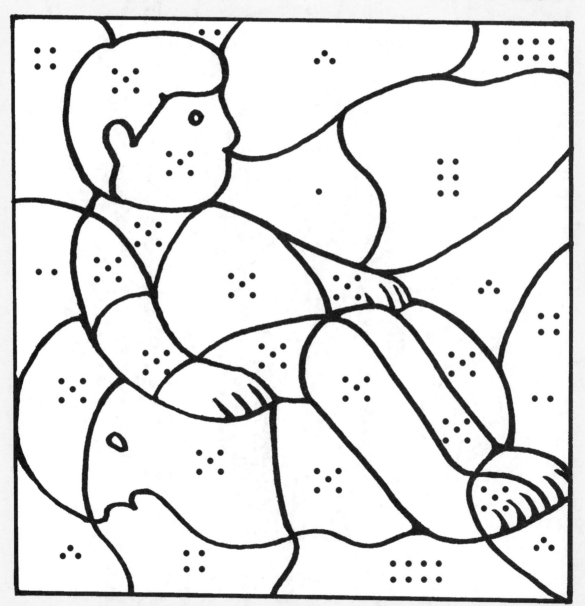

6 Six

6 shy sea horses

Practice writing the number 6.

6

Practice writing the word six.

six

Circle the group of **6**.

Circle the group of **6**.

Find the hidden picture.

Color the spaces that show **6** dots.

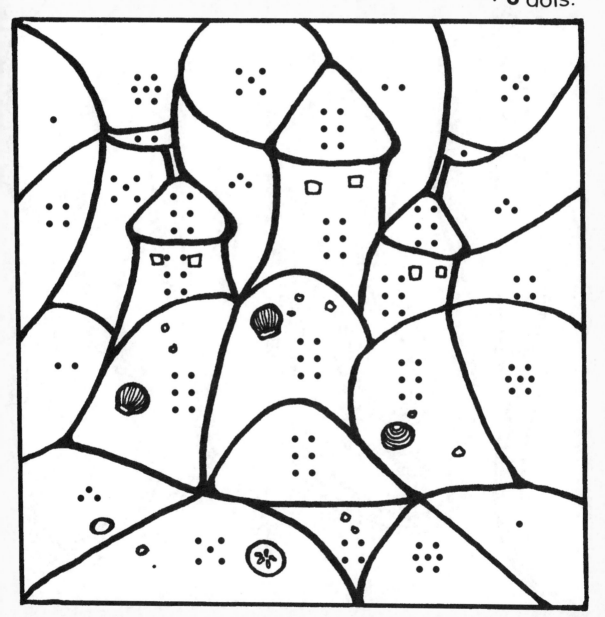

7 Seven

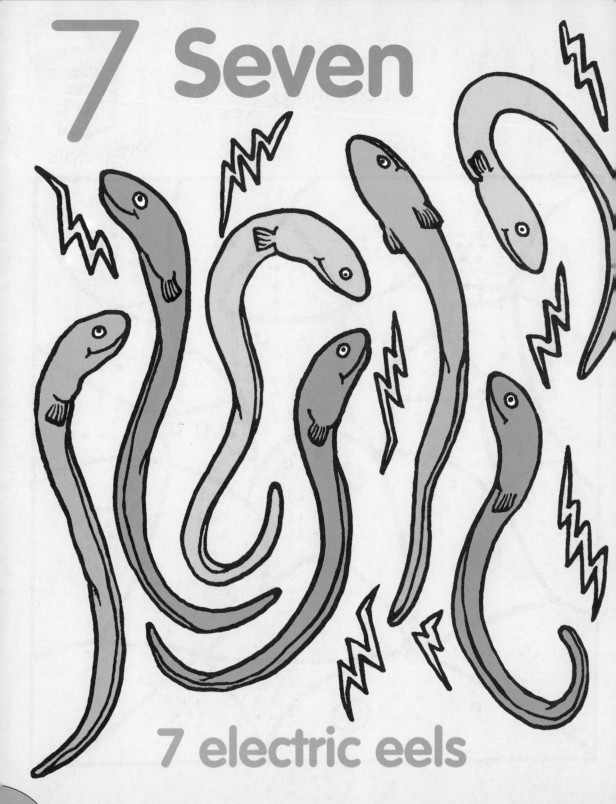

7 electric eels

Practice writing the number 7.

7

Practice writing the word **seven**.

seven

Circle the group of **7**.

Circle the group of **7**.

Find the hidden picture.

Color the spaces that show **7** dots.

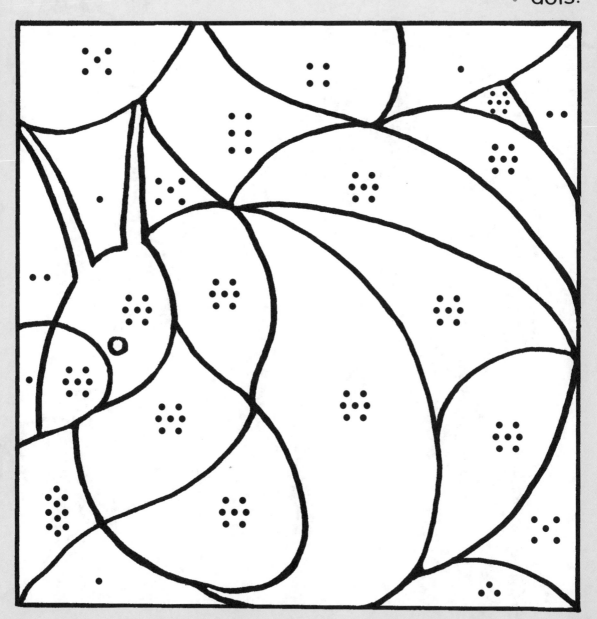

8 Eight

8 quick crabs

Practice writing the number **8**.

8

Practice writing the word **eight**.

eight

Circle the group of **8**.

Circle the group of **8**.

Find the hidden picture.

Color the spaces that show **8** dots.

9 Nine

9 quiet clams

Practice writing the number **9**.

9

Practice writing the word **nine**.

nine

Circle the group of **9**.

Circle the group of **9**.

Find the hidden picture.

Color the spaces that show **9** dots.

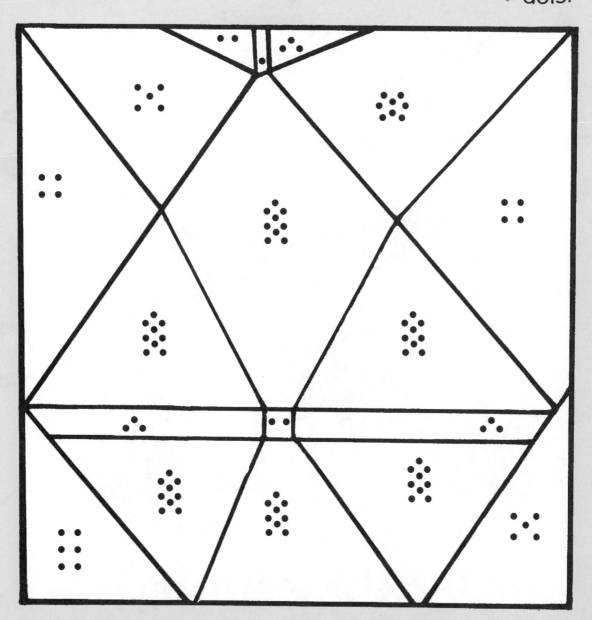

10 Ten

10 sandy starfish

40

Practice writing the number **10**.

10

Practice writing the word **ten**.

ten

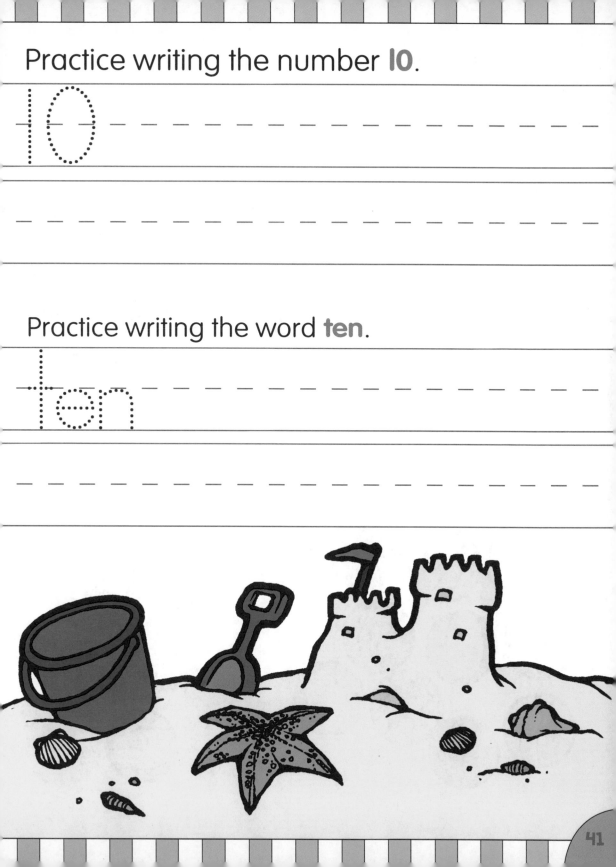

Circle the group of 10.

Circle the group of 10.

Find the hidden picture.

Color the spaces that show **10** dots.

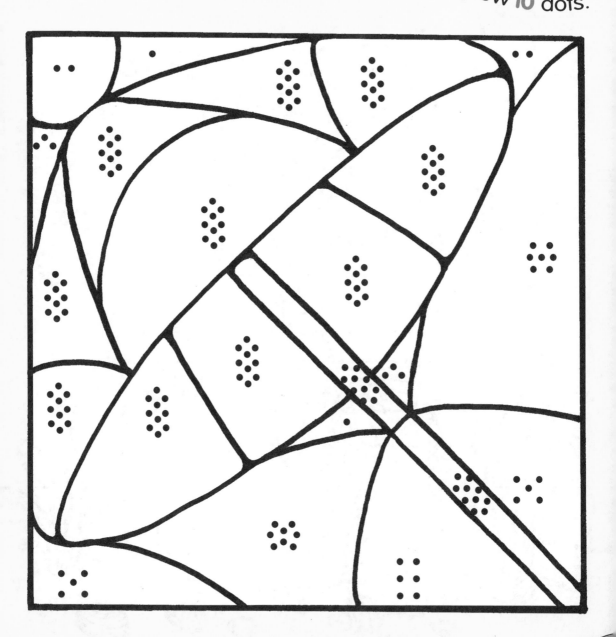

Circle 1 octopus.

Color the picture.

Circle 2 surfboards.

Color the picture.

Circle 3 snails.

Color the picture.

Circle 4 seagulls.

Color the picture.

Circle 5 crabs.

Color the picture.

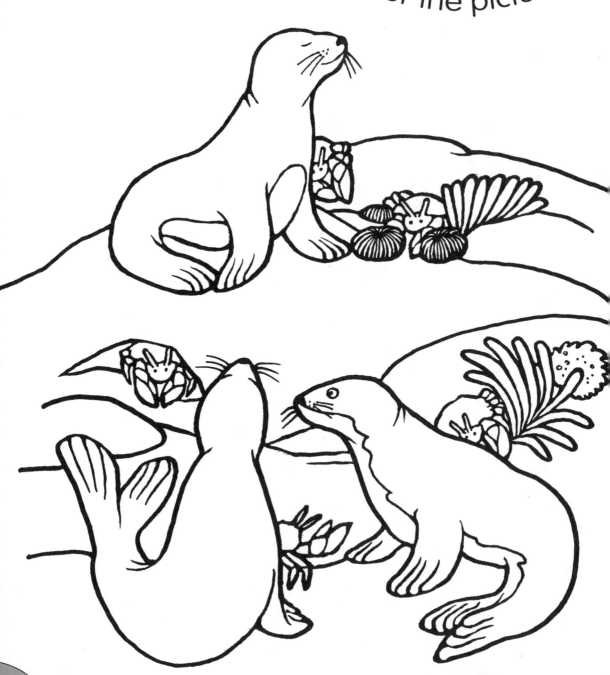

Circle 6 sea horses. Color the picture.

Circle 7 sand dollars. Color the picture

Circle 8 shells.

Color the picture.

Circle 9 fish.

Color the picture.

Circle 10 bubbles. Color the picture.

Write the missing numbers.

Count the objects. Circle the number.

8 7 9

2 3 5

4 10 9

Count the objects. Circle the number.

6 7 9

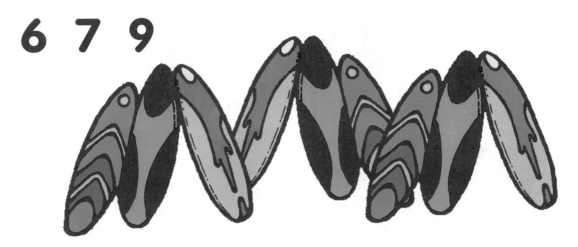

7 3 4

8 4 2

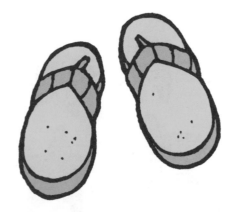

Count the objects. Circle the number.

7 4 1

2 3 5

4 6 9

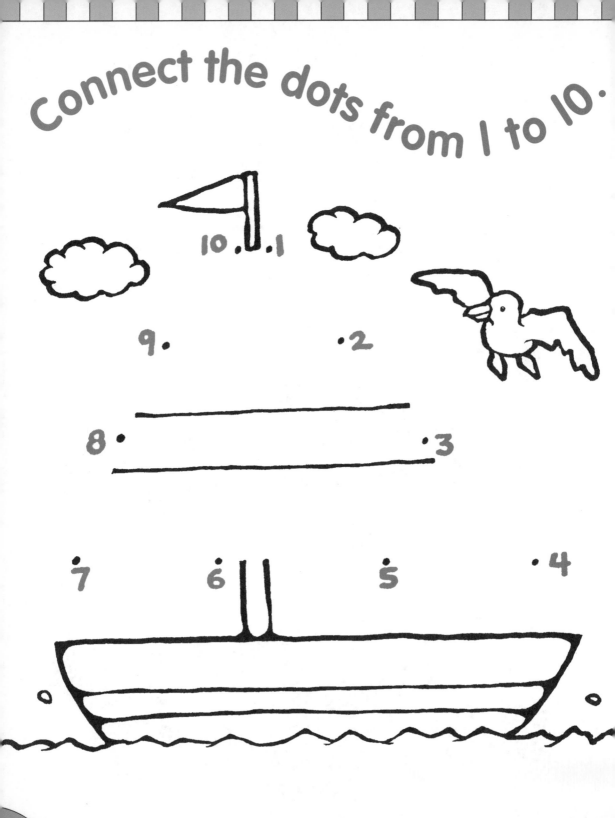

Connect the dots from 1 to 10.

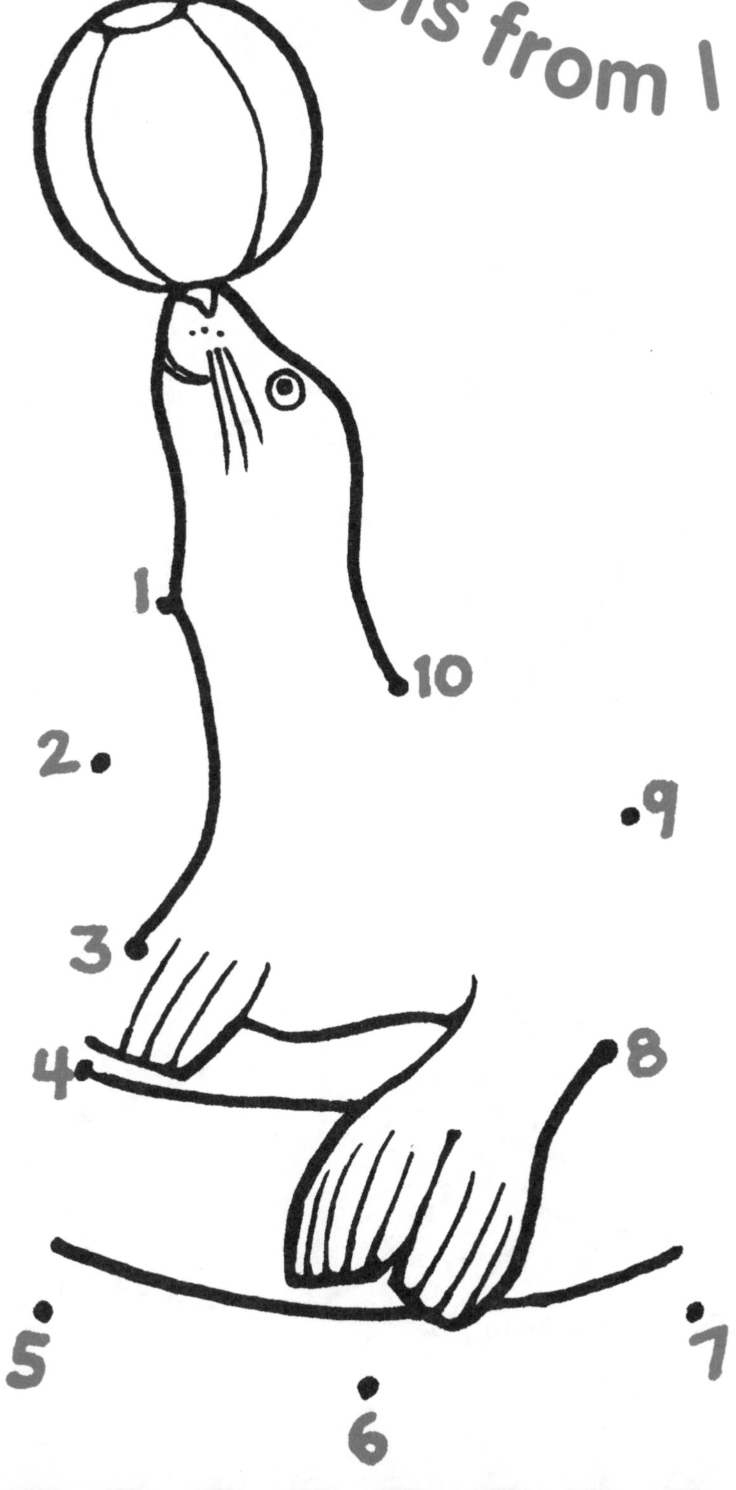

1

2.

3

4.

5

6

7

8

9

10

6

8

7

3

5

4

2

9

1

10

Connect the dots from 1 to 10.

Connect the dots from 1 to 10.

10

1

9.

8.

7

6

5

2

3

4